PERFECTIONISM
The Performance Trap

JUNE HUNT

D0188091

ROSE PUBLISHING/ASPIRE PRESS

Torrance, California

ROSE PUBLISHING/ASPIRE PRESS

CONTENTS

ear friend,

How well I remember the early years of our young ministry, when I gathered the new eager employees of HOPE FOR THE HEART for a meeting in my home. There I announced I had an important message—a must for them to remember: "I *expect* you to *make mistakes*."

Obviously, these words won't be found in any handbook for new employees. But I also recognize that people—not just our little HOPE family, but *all of us*—need the freedom to be who God created us to be—which means freedom to try and freedom to fail. So I told our team, "Don't be fearful if you make mistakes because I don't expect you to know everything. You can't know all about your job. You will make mistakes and, over a period of time, you will learn, you will grow, and you will get better."

It wasn't long before a member of our team had an opportunity to test the sincerity of my words on a grand scale. Marcie (not her real name) writes:

"I was responsible for overseeing the production of HOPE FOR THE HEART's very first informational brochure. But somehow, amid all the proofing and editing, the call letters for all the radio stations that aired our program were transposed. *None* of the call letters were correct! As a result, the brochure was completely worthless and needed to be redone. Thousands of brochures had been printed at quite a costly amount.

"June's assistant, Kay, called and said June wanted to meet with me right away. As I sat in the corner conference room, crying and wondering how in the world I could have made such a horrible mistake, I felt sure June was coming to fire me. At that moment, I looked up, through my tears, and saw her walking up the sidewalk, carrying a single yellow rose. I wasn't sure what to make of that, but felt it couldn't be a good sign.

"How wrong I was! As soon as June entered the room, she handed me the rose and began to comfort me. She acknowledged my hard work on the project, assured me that I still had my job, and reminded me again that everyone makes mistakes. Words cannot express my shock, gratitude, and relief! I worked for Hope for nearly 15 years after this happened and June never mentioned it again."

Friend, I share Marcie's story, not to shine a spotlight on myself, but to illustrate an important point taught to me by my merciful Savior.

When I look back on my own personal failures, I'm fully aware of how the Lord has continually given me both sides of the same coin: grace and mercy.

Grace means giving me a gift I *don't* deserve. It is beautifully described in Ephesians 2:8–9: *"For by grace you have been saved through faith, and that not of yourselves; it is the gift of God, not of works, lest anyone should boast"* (NKJV).

Mercy means not giving me the penalty I *do* deserve. Titus 3:5 describes it this way: *"Not by works of righteousness which we have done, but according to His mercy He saved us"* (NKJV).

Scripture exhorts us to interact gently with those who have failed: *"If someone is caught in a sin, you who live by the Spirit should restore that person gently"* (Galatians 6:1).

Knowing this is God's heart when we *sin*, imagine His tender mercy when we *make an honest mistake!* People who fall short of our expectations—and their own—don't need condemnation. They don't need harsh criticism. Instead, they need to be reassured, reaffirmed, and restored.

Though many years have passed since the founding of Hope For The Heart in 1986, I still share the same message with our new employees: "I expect you to make mistakes. I don't want you living with *a demand for perfection,* but rather *a desire for excellence.* Perfection is not the goal here, *excellence* is."

Romans 3:23 reminds us that we all *"fall short of the glory of God."* That's why Jesus lived, died and rose again! He is the only person who ever lived a perfect life. You and I never will.

So if you struggle with perfectionism, my prayer is that this book will help you re-examine your true worth in light of God's Word—a worth that's not based on "perfect performance." And as you do, may you discover God's matchless mercy and grace, and begin to freely share them with others.

Yours in the Lord's hope,

June

June Hunt

PERFECTIONISM
The Performance Trap

For perfectionists, the pressure is *always* on, and the performance *never* stops. All of life is lived under the glare of an unforgiving spotlight. The smallest blemish, the tiniest flaw, or the slightest mistake is sure to raise an eyebrow and silence sought-after acceptance.

Perfectionists are performers, but they are also prisoners chained to the opinions of others—their self-acceptance invariably linked to cherished accolades. Overlooked crumbs on the kitchen counter leave a perfectionist humiliated before guests. A student's self-worth plummets if a record of high-scoring As is broken by an unbearable B.

Even when compliments do come, such praise provides only a fleeting moment of pleasure because now the bar—the measure for self-worth—is simultaneously raised even higher.

Instead, God's plan is that we aim for *excellence*, not perfection, to accomplish our personal best with the gifts He gives us, using the power He provides.

If you are caught in the performance trap, *stop* and *rest* in the unconditional love of Christ. Stop and rest in the unconditional acceptance of our Savior. Stop your need to perform perfectly *today*. Let your last curtain call be the final curtain on performing perfectly for others.

You need to know that you are called to live for an audience of "one"—and only One—the Lord Jesus Christ, who loves and approves of you *just as you are*, crumbs on the counter and all.

Instead of living for the approval of others, you can learn to say what the apostle Paul says ...

> "We make it our goal to please him ... "
> (2 Corinthians 5:9)

DEFINITIONS

Guess who's coming to dinner!

He's a special guest, their personal friend—it's Jesus Himself. So everything *must* be perfect. Martha has invited Jesus to share a meal in her home, and she's all abuzz with her busy work. Only the best is suitable for the Prince of Peace.

Martha focuses on the menu. It must be fit for a king, but not just any king. After all, Jesus is the *King* of Kings. In addition to cooking, there's sweeping and dusting and all the other details. Martha ponders, plans, and prepares, and now upon Jesus' arrival, she's completely distracted by what's yet to be done. The Bible specifically states, *"Martha was distracted by all the preparations that had to be made"* (Luke 10:40).

No doubt—as endeared friends of Jesus—both Martha and her sister, Mary, often listened to Him speak to the multitudes. They heard Him say, *"Be perfect ... as your heavenly Father is perfect."* Did this mean He expects all of His hearers to be *sinless* in thought, *faultless* in deed, *flawless* in character?

To understand the heart of Christ on perfectionism, realize that you may need to rethink what perfection means in order to gain a biblical perspective.

Jesus, the Perfect Man, arrives at the home of His close friends Mary, Martha, and Lazarus, and the conversation is compelling. But notice the contrast: Martha fixates on food for the stomach, while Mary feasts on food for the soul.

Both have their focus on Jesus, but Martha frets over what goes *into* His mouth, while Mary focuses on comes *out of* His mouth. Mary relishes every word uttered by the Wonderful Counselor. While Martha flits, Mary *sits* at the feet of Jesus, inspiring her spirit and soul.

The diverse behavior of the two sisters prompts a lesson from Jesus about biblical *perfection*. The one scurrying in the kitchen—not the one sitting at His feet—is the one who needs the lesson. After all, Jesus said ...

> "I tell you, do not worry about ...
> what you will eat or drink. ...
> Is not life more than food?"
> (Matthew 6:25)

Two Different Distinctions

THE CONTEMPORARY CONNOTATION

▶ **Perfection** means being faultless, flawless, sinless, entirely without error—free from defect.[1]

- The Bible describes God in this way: *"As for God, his way is perfect: The Lord's word is flawless ..."* (2 Samuel 22:31).

- The Bible describes Jesus in this way: *"... the Son, who has been made perfect forever"* (Hebrews 7:28).

THE BIBLICAL CONNOTATION

Spiritually Mature

▶ **Perfection** means being mature and complete—blameless (incontestable in character) and "righteous"[2] (right in God's sight). God has provided all that is necessary for you to walk righteously—in a way that is right in God's sight.

- **"Perfect"** is the word used to describe Noah's complete maturity.[3]

  "Noah was a just man, perfect in his generations. Noah walked with God" (Genesis 6:9 NKJV).

- **"Perfection"** is what Paul prayed for—that all believers would achieve complete maturity.

  "This is what we pray for, that you may become perfect" (2 Corinthians 13:9 NRSV).

- **Perfection** is what Paul admitted he had not attained, but what Christ planned for him to achieve—complete maturity.

  "Not that I have already attained, or am already perfected; but I press on, that I may lay hold of that for which Christ Jesus has also laid hold of me" (Philippians 3:12 NKJV).

Spiritually Complete

▶ **Perfection** means "complete, finished, whole."[4]

  ▪ **Perfect unity** is what Jesus prayed for—that all believers would experience complete unity of love.

  "... *that they may become perfectly one, so that the world may know that you sent me and loved them even as you loved me*" (John 17:23 ESV).

  ▪ **"Perfect peace"** is spoken of by Isaiah—that God gives complete peace to those who steadily entrust their lives to the Lord.

  "*You will keep in perfect peace those whose minds are steadfast, because they trust in you*" (Isaiah 26:3).

Aim for Excellence

QUESTION: "Since the Bible says, *'Be perfect'* (2 Corinthians 13:11 KJV), aren't we literally called to be sinless?"

ANSWER: God understands that all humans—even faithful Christians—make mistakes and sin. The biblical word "perfect" typically means "mature and complete" as we surrender our will to God's will. Therefore, we are called to be perfect—not faultless, sinless, flawless—but rather be perfect—mature, whole, complete.

The Bible addresses this truth—that at times we all sin: "*If we claim to be without sin, we deceive ourselves and the truth is not in us*" (1 John 1:8).

As Jesus visits His faithful friends, Martha's eyes become fixated on the reclining figure on the floor—her sister, simply sitting at the feet of Jesus. Resentment rears its ugly head and takes root in Martha's heart.

In essence, Martha is fuming in front of Jesus. "How can Mary just sit there when there is so much to be done? Mary isn't helping at all! No one's helping me. No one notices my perfect efforts to make the perfect meal in our perfectly clean home."

Martha decides that Jesus needs to do something about this! She's determined to get Mary up off the floor and into the kitchen. So rather than appeal to Mary, Martha challenges Jesus' insensitivity. As she chastizes Him for being uncaring, her words are saturated with self-pity: *"Lord, don't you care that my sister has left me to do the work by myself?"*

Then, propelled by her perfectionism, Martyr Martha audaciously commands the Commander of the universe: *"Tell her to help me!"* (Luke 10:40).

Many people today are propelled by their perfectionism—to their personal detriment.

▶ **Perfectionism** is an unhealthy, compulsive pattern of thinking that demands perfection in any undertaking.

- Anything less than perfect is unacceptable.

- No task is attempted unless perfection is attainable.

For example, Jesus tells the parable of the talents—money given to three men by their master to invest wisely. This consisted of eight talents—or eight pounds of gold—with each talent the equivalent of about 20 years' worth of wages. While two servants doubled their investment, the third man hid his gold and said, *"I was afraid and went out and hid your gold in the ground. See, here is what belongs to you"* (Matthew 25:25).

▶ **Perfectionists** appear confident, conscientious, and highly productive, but the truth is ...

- They are full of self-doubt and fear that the slightest mistake or misstep will cause others to be disappointed in them or reject them.

- They become overly sensitive to the opinions and feedback of others, often disregarding their own healthy instincts.

The Bible says, *"People look at the outward appearance, but the LORD looks at the heart"* (1 Samuel 16:7).

▶ **Perfectionists** live in an overly cautious way.

- They are reluctant to try new tasks, take risks, or tackle big projects.

- They fear failing or appearing "inadequate" in the eyes of others.

The Bible says, *"Be strong in the Lord and in his mighty power"* (Ephesians 6:10).

"Martha, Martha ... " Not once, but twice Jesus speaks her name, perceiving her unnecessary angst. Then He poignantly addresses her problematic perfectionism: *"You are worried and upset about many things, but few things are needed—or indeed only one. Mary has chosen what is better, and it will not be taken away from her"* (Luke 10:41–42).

Stop "doing"! Only one dish is really needed. Jesus makes it clear: Martha must follow Mary's example—not the reverse—to sit and partake of food that will never perish. Even today, Jesus says to us ...

> **"Do not work for food that spoils,**
> **but for food that endures to eternal life,**
> **which the Son of Man will give you."**
> **(John 6:27)**

Below are a few unhealthy patterns of perfectionism you may recognize.

▶ **Legalism** is a strict adherence to religious rules and regulations with the false hope of earning righteousness

Example: "If I don't keep the dietary law of my church, I'll be doomed."

But the Bible says, *"Do not let anyone judge you by what you eat or drink, or with regard to a religious festival, a New Moon celebration or a Sabbath day"* (Colossians 2:16).

▶ **Performance-based acceptance** is a belief that acceptance by God and others is based only on how much is achieved and how perfectly actions are performed

Example: "I must achieve great success in order for God and others to accept me."

But the Bible says, *"I will expose your righteousness and your works, and they will not benefit you"* (Isaiah 57:12).

▶ **Obsessive Compulsive Disorder** is an unhealthy, emotional imbalance characterized by persistent, excessive thoughts and inflexible, irrational behavior often in a drive for perfection[5]

Example: "I must wash my hands again and again before I can ever enjoy eating."

But the Bible says, *" ... eating with unwashed hands does not defile them"* (Matthew 15:20).

When your desire for excellence turns into a demand for perfection, your thinking and behavior become governed by relentless rules that are excessive, detrimental, and out of the will of God.

In the Bible, the Lord describes these kinds of rule keepers ...

"These people come near to me with their mouth and honor me with their lips, but their hearts are far from me. Their worship of me is based on merely human rules they have been taught." (Isaiah 29:13)

Legalism vs. Performance-Based Acceptance

QUESTION: "Is performance-based acceptance related to legalism, and what is the ultimate solution?"

ANSWER: There is definitely a relationship, especially since legalism is the platform on which performance-based acceptance stands.

▶ *Legalism* means living under the law and requiring obedience to the law. The concept is: Keep "the law" and you will be accepted; break "the law" and you will be rejected.

▶ *Performance-based acceptance* means performing according to "the law of another person" in order to be accepted. Under the performance-based acceptance system, acceptance is based totally on performance.

▶ *Grace*, the solution, means receiving undeserved salvation as a gift from God and then living free of the law and its stringent requirements. Grace is the platform on which "acceptance-based performance" stands.

▶ *Acceptance-based performance* means doing what is right to please the Lord based on gratitude for being totally accepted by God. Under the acceptance-based performance system, the motivation for doing what is right is based on having already received God's love and acceptance. *"We love because he first loved us"* (1 John 4:19).

"Mary has chosen what is better ... " (Luke 10:42).

But what is better? Striving toward spiritual maturity, seeking to better understand God's divine purposes for your life is the far more noble endeavor, according to Jesus. The desire for excellence trumps the demand for perfection, and there is no way Jesus is going to let Martha prevent Mary's pursuit.

And so it is with your life—just as Martha was consumed with multiple duties and perfect dishes, are you consumed with multiple projects or perfect meals to impress certain people? Are you constantly performing, constantly doing to gain acceptance and approval?

Though many miss the point of Jesus' teachings, those who do understand know what is most important to do—to sit at His feet.

And Simon Peter explains why ...

"Lord ... You have the words of eternal life."
(John 6:68)

► **Excellence is achieving** your personal best in order to be all God created you to be.

  ▪ You can excel in the areas based on your unique God-given gifts and talents.

  ▪ The apostle Paul said, *"I will show you the most excellent way"* (1 Corinthians 12:31). Then he spends an entire chapter describing the way of love (1 Corinthians 13).

► **Excellence is living** your life in a way that is over and above the average.

  ▪ You can exceed and surpass the ordinary.

  ▪ We are told to *" ... try to excel in those* [gifts] *that build up the church"* (1 Corinthians 14:12).

Challenging yourself to meet the reasonable, reachable standards of excellence is healthy. Problems arise only when your desire for excellence becomes a demand for perfection—goals that go beyond reason and reach. God desires that you strive for attainable excellence so that we will reflect His values and principles.

As the Bible stresses ...

"This is a trustworthy saying.
And I want you to stress these things,
so that those who have trusted in God may
be careful to devote themselves to doing
what is good. These things are excellent
and profitable for everyone."
(Titus 3:8)

Perfectionistic Professionals

QUESTION: "Doesn't every doctor, dentist, or other professional need to be a perfectionist?"

ANSWER: No. When new approaches are needed, perfectionists are often less flexible or less likely to try new ideas or procedures. They are typically too fear-based to try new approaches. The most successful and talented professionals push themselves toward excellence, not perfection. No matter what your occupation, you are to do your work as though you are working for the Lord.

> "Whatever you do, work at it with all
> your heart, as working for the Lord,
> not for human masters."
> (Colossians 3:23)

Superheroes exist in culture after culture—fictitious figures with superhuman strength, blighted with human frailties, but filled with compassion for the weak and defenseless, the victims of self-centered super villains. Heroes are created out of our common need to have someone who won't take advantage of our universally shared imperfections—someone who will meet us at our point of need, stand in the gap, take up our cause, and make everything right.

Typically, those who have not found the real God of the Bible and have not established a personal relationship with Him either seek an imagined superhero or seek to become their own hero—they seek to become perfect! The problem? No one can consistently excel in every area of life; therefore, self-imposed standards soon collapse, leaving discouragement and dejection in their wake.

God's heart is for every person to grasp His message of grace, His message of mercy, and to know His truth in order to experience freedom from the prison of perfectionism.

> **"You will know the truth,**
> **and the truth will set you free."**
> **(John 8:32)**

Freedom for the Perfectionist

Freedom from perfectionism begins at the point of truth. Regularly repeating these 10 messages will set the wheels of change in motion in your life.

Message #1

▶ "I don't always have to measure up because no one is perfect."

▶ The Bible says, *"All have sinned and fall short of the glory of God"* (Romans 3:23).

Message #2

▶ "I never have to fear losing God's love due to anything I might or might not do because His love is unconditional."

▶ The Bible says, *"I am convinced that neither death nor life, neither angels nor demons, neither the present nor the future, nor any powers, neither height nor depth, nor anything else in all creation, will be able to separate us from the love of God that is in Christ Jesus our Lord"* (Romans 8:38–39).

Message #3

▶ "I have a clear conscience and am free from guilt and regret over past failures because I have been forgiven by God and have been given the righteousness of Christ."

▶ The Bible says, *"Forget the former things; do not dwell on the past. See, I am doing a new thing! Now it springs up; do you not perceive it? I am making a way in the wilderness and streams in the wasteland"* (Isaiah 43:18–19).

Message #4

▶ "I can live without fear of being condemned even when I fail to meet the expectations of others because God has accepted me in Christ."

▶ The Bible says, *"The Spirit you received does not make you slaves, so that you live in fear again; rather, the Spirit you received brought about your adoption to sonship. And by him we cry, 'Abba, Father'"* (Romans 8:15).

Message #5

▶ "I can stop comparing myself to others because God designed me to be a unique, one-of-a-kind person."

▶ The Bible says, *"I praise you because I am fearfully and wonderfully made; your works are wonderful, I know that full well"* (Psalm 139:14).

Message #6

▶ "I can confidently take on new challenges because with Christ in me I'm not limited to doing only those things at which I excel."

▶ The Bible says, *"The LORD will be your confidence and will keep your foot from being caught"* (Proverbs 3:26 ESV).

Message #7

▶ "I don't have to worry about finding the perfect job or selecting the ideal situation because I can trust God to prepare the way for my future."

▶ The Bible says, *"We are God's handiwork, created in Christ Jesus to do good works, which God prepared in advance for us to do"* (Ephesians 2:10).

Message #8

▶ "I am free to enjoy life because God has freed me from bondage to a set of rules and regulations."

▶ The Bible says, *"If the Son sets you free, you will be free indeed"* (John 8:36).

Message #9

▶ "My salvation is a free gift because it's not based on what I deserve or earn through my work or other achievements."

▶ The Bible says, *"He* [God] *has saved us ... not because of anything we have done but because of his own purpose and grace"* (2 Timothy 1:9).

Message #10

▶ "God does not expect me to become Christlike in my own power because God assumes responsibility for bringing me to maturity."

▶ The Bible says, *"being confident of this, that he who began a good work in you will carry it on to completion ... "* (Philippians 1:6).

CHARACTERISTICS OF PERFECTIONISTS

Anne Smith, ten-time Grand Slam doubles tennis champion, was the world's top-ranked female doubles player in 1980 and 1981. Competing against the best names in tennis, including Martina Navratilova and Billie Jean King, she captured two Wimbledon crowns, three U.S. Open titles, four French Open championships, and many other prestigious wins.[6]

Not only an accomplished tennis player, she also became Dr. Anne Smith—licensed psychologist. Then she won a new title: "recovering perfectionist."

The essential feature of perfectionism is compulsive behavior resulting from a need borne out of insecurity, a need to "go above and beyond the call of duty." Instead of joyfully giving out of love, the perfectionist gives out of duty in an effort to please others. Such a desperate need for the approval of others is often rooted in fear and misplaced trust—a treacherous trap, as the Bible reveals ...

**"Fear of man will prove to be a snare,
but whoever trusts in the LORD is kept safe."
(Proverbs 29:25)**

Anne Smith's mind-set during much of her professional tennis career was muddied—by the missed shot.[7] "During my career in the 1980s, my perfectionism fueled my anger and caused me to feel as if I were fighting myself instead of my opponent." Anne considered herself her "own worst enemy," and often couldn't even enjoy the game in which she received one accolade after another because *mistakes* monopolized her thoughts. She later realized that a laser focus on mistakes leads to something else—*more mistakes.*

When she dusted off her racket in 2005 and returned to the professional circuit—sometimes challenging opponents 20 to 30 years her junior—Dr. Anne Smith was determined to do things *differently.* "I have given up the idea that I cannot miss, or that I have to be perfect. ... Focusing on what I am doing well helps create a winning mind-set and enhances my performance. It is also much more fun."

In 2007, Dr. Smith celebrated yet another victory on the court mixed doubles champion at the U.S. Open Champions Invitational.

However, those who have not yet moved past this mental malady continually live with the unspoken creed of the perfectionist: "Anything worth doing is worth doing *perfectly.*"

Notice the sharp contrast of these words compared to those of King Solomon, called by God the wisest man who ever lived ...

> "Yet when I surveyed all that my hands had done and what I had toiled to achieve, everything was meaningless ... " (Ecc. 2:11)

The Profile of a Perfectionist

You have perfectionistic tendencies if typically you ...

▶ **Maintain** a black-or-white, all-or-nothing view of life

Example: "If I don't succeed at this, I am a true failure."

▶ **Set** impossibly high goals and then strive to achieve them

Example: "I must never make a mistake," or "I will always win high praise."

▶ **Become** overly concerned with what others think of you, fearing you may lose respect, status, or favor if you are "exposed" as being imperfect

Example: "No one would accept me if I were known for who I really am."

▶ **Feel** upset by the smallest mistake, especially when someone else points it out

Example: "I will never have credibility after making such a stupid mistake."

▶ **Compare** your weaker skills to the finest traits and talents of others

Example: "Why can't I be as good as they are?"

▶ **Minimize** your God-given gifts and agonize over areas of lesser natural ability

Example: "I can't measure up in areas where it really matters."

▶ **Find** fault with others, feeling frustrated because they don't meet your standards

Example: "Why can't people just do what I ask without making mistakes?"

▶ **Think** that what you have accomplished is never good enough

Example: "I still should have done better."

▶ **Procrastinate**, feeling intimidated that it might not come out perfectly

Example: "I can't start this assignment until I have everything needed to do it perfectly."

Those who want to be considered "recovered perfectionists" must have a change of heart with a change of goals. This means giving up the goal of winning the approval of people and replacing it with the desire to be a servant of Christ, as this Scripture indicates ...

"Am I now trying to win the approval of human beings, or of God? Or am I trying to please people? If I were still trying to please people, I would not be a servant of Christ."
(Galatians 1:10)

Checklist of a Classic Perfectionist

Is it possible that you are a perfectionist? Do you continually strive to have everything perfect? Have you ever wished that you could just be you, and then find out whether you are really accepted by others—warts and all? Place a check mark (✓) beside each question that applies to you.

Do you ...

☐ Allow your perception of what others might think of you rob you of contentment?

☐ Anticipate that other people are always trying to find fault with you?

☐ Assume you must please everyone all the time?

☐ Avoid conflict at all costs, believing that if there is conflict you must have done something wrong?

☐ Believe if you are less than perfect, then you can lose your salvation?

☐ Conclude that you are responsible for the behavior of others?

☐ Consider mistakes to never be permissible?

☐ Establish goals so high that you continually stress over trying to achieve them?

☐ Expect people close to you to know what you want without telling them?

☐ Feel responsible for everyone else's happiness?

- ☐ Find it impossible to let go of a mistake?
- ☐ Hold back and not take any risks because you are afraid of failure?
- ☐ Need to have everything in its place—always?
- ☐ Presume you must perform perfectly in order to gain and keep God's love?
- ☐ Put all of your energy into living life to please others?
- ☐ Question whether people would still love you if they really knew you?
- ☐ Set a higher standard for yourself than you do for others?
- ☐ Spend more time trying to be who you think others think you are, rather than just being who you truly are?
- ☐ Suppose that making a mistake diminishes your value?
- ☐ Take for granted that others think the way you think?
- ☐ Think people judge you if your house isn't immaculate?
- ☐ Wonder why everyone doesn't act the same way you do ... because your way is the "right" way?

If you find that you identify with the perfectionist, take the following words of Jesus to heart:

> "Come to me, all you who are weary and burdened, and I will give you rest."
> (Matthew 11:28)

Procrastination

QUESTION: "I used to be a perfectionist who accomplished so much, but now I can't even get to work on time or get my work finished. Why am I constantly procrastinating?"

ANSWER: A perfectionist often procrastinates because "fear of failure" takes control of emotions and paralyzes productivity. Perfectionists seek to get their need for significance met through excellent work, but perfectionism is an impossible goal to maintain. The time eventually comes when the work is never quite good enough, and it seems better to do nothing than to risk feeling like a failure. If you are serious about moving beyond perfection-driven procrastination ...

▶ **Change** your goal from seeking to please others to earn acceptance and begin trusting the Lord for His unconditional acceptance.

▶ **Realize** that your significance comes from Christ, residing in you, not from any of your accomplishments.

▶ **View** your work as being given by the Lord as an opportunity to allow His wisdom and power to operate within you and through you to accomplish His purposes.

▶ **Focus** on pleasing the Lord in all you do with a heart of genuine gratitude.

The Bible says, *"Serve wholeheartedly, as if you were serving the Lord, not people"* (Ephesians 6:7).

Serious tennis players like Dr. Anne Smith typically use a tennis ball machine to improve their skills. After being loaded with 100 to 300 balls, this machine shoots balls at the speeds of 15 to 95 miles per hour for players to hit back.

The balls automatically sail across the net with topspin or backspin at whatever height, speed, or direction chosen—all based on what has been programmed into the machine.

In a similar way, the obsessive thoughts of perfectionists can pound away like a barrage of high-speed balls, hurling intrusive thoughts, one after another. And the *compulsive acts* of perfectionists are similar to a tennis player who feels compelled to hit every high-speed ball—but her swing must be perfectly controlled. However, unlike with the tennis ball machine, the perfectionist seemingly has no control.

The psalmist laments ...

"How long must I wrestle with my thoughts and day after day have sorrow in my heart?"
(Psalm 13:2)

The Compulsive Person's Profile

Perfectionism and compulsiveness go hand in hand. Those who demand perfection are often driven by obsessive thoughts and compulsive traits. As a result of feeling powerless to control their obsessions and compulsions, these perfectionists ...

▶ **Need** to control their environment, circumstances, or other people.

- They must be in control to override feelings of fear and insecurity and to make sure things go well.

▶ **Object** to criticism and correction

- They react defensively to any suggestion that they might be less than competent to perform a task perfectly.

▶ **Major** on the minors

- They become preoccupied with trivial details to avoid necessary tasks because of a fear of failure.

▶ **Procrastinate** when faced with projects and deadlines

- They put off starting projects because of a fear of inadequacy to perform a task perfectly.

▶ **Underestimate** time needed to complete tasks

- They tend to overcommit because of an unrealistic view of personal limitations and the driving need to prove their personal worth.

▶ **Lose** their sense of joy and creativity

- They reveal inflexibility when it comes to trying new ideas or changing the way tasks are performed for fear of making mistakes.

▶ **Sacrifice** relationships for projects

- They prioritize task-driven projects to the detriment of nurturing relationships.

▶ **Assume** rejection from others

- They expect to receive disapproval from people because they disapprove of themselves and consider themselves unworthy of being valued.

▶ **Don't** like to make decisions

- They avoid or postpone making decisions out of fear of making wrong decisions.

▶ **Express** intolerance toward others

- They become impatient with peoples' mistakes, viewing others as inferior for their lower standards.

Perfectionists seem highly motivated to produce, yet their behavior is actually a compulsive drive to protect themselves from feeling condemned.[8] They live under a legalistic law (seeking to earn approval) instead of living under the grace of God (accepting unearned approval). They need to take to heart this truth shared by the apostle Paul: *"There is now no condemnation for those who are in Christ Jesus, because through Christ Jesus the law of the Spirit who gives life has set you free from the law of sin and death"* (Romans 8:1–2).

Perfectionist Anne Smith brought her addiction to achievement to the tennis court in the same way that Coach Jimmy Johnson brought his "achievement addiction" to the football field.

Johnson spearheaded the University of Miami's football team to a national collegiate championship in 1987, then led the world renown Dallas Cowboys to two Super Bowl titles in 1992 and 1993. All great accomplishments—all attained at a great cost.[9]

As a self-described achievement addict, Johnson regularly worked 16 hours a day to prepare for weekly football games. He routinely missed his children's birthday celebrations. Time with his wife was basically limited to touching elbows at public appearances and social events.

Perfectionists who prioritize projects over people are achievement addicts who would not only be challenged by this Scripture but would also be helped—if applied ...

"... not looking to your own interests but each of you to the interests of the others."
(Philippians 2:4)

The Achievement Addicts Checklist

Place a check mark (✓) by each question that applies to you. If you or someone close to you thinks you might be a compulsive worker, honestly evaluate whether the following questions apply to you.

☐ Do I believe my work is the main source of my identity?

☐ Do I dive into details and lists but have difficulty starting essentials?

☐ Do I have difficulty pacing my time?

☐ Do I have difficulty being satisfied with the final result?

☐ Do I feel my work is controlling me?

☐ Do I make sure others know how much and how long I work?

☐ Do I resent others for not working as hard as I think they should?

☐ Do I feel guilty when I relax or have fun?

☐ Do I often feel fatigued due to work?

☐ Do I prioritize work above those closest to me?

☐ Do I talk primarily about my work-related activities?

☐ Do I fear that others might think I don't work hard enough?

☐ Do I have difficulty saying *no*?

☐ Do I think the more I work, the more I will please God?

☐ Do I show more devotion to my work than to God?

If you marked *yes* to many of these questions, it might help you to know what the wisest man who ever lived said about his own work, which he knew was misprioritized ...

> **"My heart began to despair over all my toilsome labor under the sun."**
> **(Ecclesiastes 2:20)**

An achievement addict is a person who is compulsively addicted to work to the detriment of self and significant relationships. Sadly, there are achievement addicts in every workplace.

And for these compulsive achievers the "top rung" is always the target because their self-image is measured by what they *do*, not by who they *are*. Projects, not personal relationships, are what matter most to these perfectionists. They are driven to outsmart, outmatch, and outrank in order to attain the coveted label—*outstanding!*

For those who "need to be known," those who seek glory, they need to know that glory is due to the Lord alone.

> **"I am the LORD; that is my name!**
> **I will not yield my glory to another ... "**
> **(Isaiah 42:8)**

Compulsive behavior takes its toll physically. Because the mind, body, and spirit are connected, an addiction to perfectionism may result in negative consequences to health and well-being. Tennis pro Anne Smith and football coach Jimmy Johnson learned the hard way about the negative impact of a perfectionist mind-set—affecting not only her physical performance on the court but also her emotional well-being off the court.

These words from the Psalms reflect the plight of the perfectionist: *"My spirit grows faint within me; my heart within me is dismayed"* (Psalm 143:4).

Some of the physical consequences connected to perfectionism and overachievement include ...

▶ Angry outbursts

▶ Arthritis

▶ Back pain

▶ Chest tightness

▶ Chronic fatigue

▶ Cold sores

▶ Depression

▶ Difficulty relaxing

▶ Dizziness

▶ Eating disorders

▶ Headaches

▶ Heart disease

▶ High blood pressure

▶ Hives

▶ Muscle tension

▶ Sleep disturbance

▶ Stomach problems

▶ Sore jaws as a result of grinding teeth

Efforts to earn God's approval or the consistent approval of others is ultimately a fruitless endeavor, as the apostle Paul discovered ...

> "I found that the very commandment
> that was intended to bring
> life actually brought death."
> (Romans 7:10)

WHAT CHARACTERIZES
Perfectionism vs. Excellence?

The differences between the demand for perfection and the desire for excellence are significant. The perfectionist not only fails to rely on God, but also places trust in self-effort. The Bible calls this sin ...

> "Those who trust in themselves
> are fools, but those who
> walk in wisdom are kept safe."
> (Proverbs 28:26)

Rather than rely on himself, the apostle Paul gave all the credit to God for his works ...

> "But whatever I am now it is all because God
> poured out such kindness and grace upon
> me—and not without results:
> for I have worked harder than all the other
> apostles, yet actually I wasn't doing it,
> but God working in me, to bless me"
> (1 Corinthians 15:10 TLB).

The Demand for Perfection Declares	The Desire for Excellence Declares
My best isn't good enough.	I am pleased with my best.
I have to get a promotion.	I hope to get a promotion.
I must keep a spotless house.	I want to keep a clean house.
I must make top grades.	I would like to make straight As.
It must be the best if I give it my best.	It may not be the best, but I'll give it my best.
I hate being average in any area.	I feel fairly competent in several areas.
I must do better than anyone else.	I did better than I've ever done.
There's nothing worse than being a failure.	Failure is a part of life, and I can learn important lessons from my mistakes.
I have to do better.	I would like to do better.
I feel frustrated after doing this work.	I feel fulfilled after doing this work.
I'll be perfect if I try hard enough.	I hope to excel when I give it my best.

The Demand for Perfection Declares	The Desire for Excellence Declares
I dread starting this big project—I can't guarantee a perfect outcome.	I'll enjoy starting this big project, breaking it into manageable parts—I'll desire a positive outcome.
I'll prioritize fulfilling my duties perfectly.	I'll prioritize fulfilling God's purpose for me.
I can't be content if it's not perfect.	I'll be content to do my best.

The person desiring excellence realizes ...

"Godliness with contentment is great gain."
(1 Timothy 6:6)

42

WHAT CHARACTERIZES the Idealist vs. the Realist?

Perfectionists are often idealists who reach for unreachable stars and pursue impossible dreams. They lack the practicality that accompanies realism and therefore experience disappointment after disappointment and heartbreak after heartbreak when the ideal job or relationship never materializes. They identify with the words of Job: *"My days have passed, my plans are shattered. Yet the desires of my heart turn night into day ... "* (Job 17:11–12).

THE IDEALIST	THE REALIST
Demands success	Desires success
Dwells on mistakes	Learns from mistakes
Fears failure	Accepts failure
Defends when criticized	Profits when criticized
Focuses on the end product and the results that must be accomplished	Focuses on the process, enjoying how the task is accomplished
Despises losing, feels unacceptable	Doesn't like losing but still feels acceptable

The realist can say with the apostle Paul, *"I glory in Christ Jesus in my service to God. I will not venture to speak of anything except what Christ has accomplished through me ... "* (Romans 15:17–18).

CAUSES OF BECOMING A PERFECTIONIST

Perfectionist parents took a toll on the sixth president of the United States.[11]

The oldest boy in the family, John Quincy Adams bore the responsibility of carrying on his family's rich heritage and honor—and his parents never let him forget it. As a little boy he was often told that he was expected to become a "great man." He was expected to set an example of proper moral conduct for his siblings and to one day distinguish himself by setting an example of sacrificial service for his fellow countrymen. Little "Johnny" had big shoes to fill after all, his father was the second president of the United States.

To drive home the high cost of freedom and service, Johnny's mother, Abigail, made him watch soldiers fall at the Battle of Bunker Hill, including witnessing the death of a beloved family friend. A traumatic lesson taught to him at the tender age of seven.

How does one become a perfectionist? As was the case of young John Quincy Adams, the seeds for perfectionism are often sown in childhood. Children who are loved, appreciated, or acknowledged only *conditionally* (with "strings attached") learn to value themselves on the basis of performance and the approval of others. Similarly, children whose parents harshly scold, punish, or shame them for failing to behave "perfectly" learn to fear mistakes—and go to great lengths to hide their human imperfections.

Sadly, such children clearly identify with the words of the psalmist ...

"I live in disgrace all day long, and my face is covered with shame at the taunts of those who reproach and revile me ... "
(Psalm 44:15–16)

WHAT ARE Situational Setups for Perfectionists?

Johnny's parents issued tall orders for such a young boy.[12] And when John Quincy Adams couldn't reach the high bar of achievement, he seemingly was always cut down to size. His young, impressionable mind absorbed the constant barrage of parental expectations placed on him. And his self-image was molded by the crushing repercussions of the slightest failure. No wonder he transitioned from a shy, insecure boy into an introverted adult. No wonder he became his own worst critic and suffered days of discouragement and depression.

How different his mind-set would have been had his parents heeded the Lord's instruction ...

"Fathers, do not embitter your children, or they will become discouraged."
(Colossians 3:21)

Perfectionists continually strive for acceptance because the acceptance they received in the past was based on how well they performed, how well they followed the dictates and fulfilled the desires of others. If parents or other significant people in your childhood gave you approval only for achievement, the message you received was a setup for perfectionism.

To curb the setup for perfectionism, parents would do well to mirror these words of Scripture ...

"But you, O Lord, are a God merciful and gracious, slow to anger and abounding in steadfast love and faithfulness."
(Psalm 86:15 ESV)

If you struggle with perfectionism or achievement addiction, evaluate your situational setup by reflecting on the parenting style practiced in your family and the messages derived from what you experienced.

Situational Setups[13]

▶ **Perfectionistic Parents**

- **Message received by children**: "I must be the best at everything I do."

  Performance is the idol worshiped in homes where perfectionism is enshrined. Value and worth are defined by how well children measure up, and only high achievers win the "crown of acceptance."

- **However**, straining always to be the best is unnecessary. You have intrinsic value for who you are, apart from what you do.

"Look at the birds of the air; they do not sow or reap or store away in barns, and yet your heavenly Father feeds them. Are you not much more valuable than they?" (Matthew 6:26).

▶ **Achievement-Addicted Parents**

- **Message received by children**: "Work is the most important thing."

Since children generally adopt the values of their authority figures, work reigns as king among children of parents who are addicted to achievement. Meaning and purpose appear to be identical twins of being successful and productive. All else, including relationships, pale in comparison.

- **However**, though work can be meaningful, it must not take precedence over more important priorities.

"It is senseless for you to work so hard from early morning until late at night, fearing you will starve to death; for God wants his loved ones to get their proper rest" (Psalm 127:2 TLB).

▶ **Alcoholic Parents**

- **Message received by children**: "Someone in the family has to take charge."

Children of alcoholics experience chaos and insecurity in their homes, thus causing them to seek control as the family "manager." They take charge of their circumstances and assume responsibility for the family image. Everything depends on them, so they cannot afford to be less than perfect.

- **However**, those who take on the responsibilities of others may think they are doing what is right, but much is lost, including trust, respect, security, and often the premature end of childhood.

"Then Jesus said, 'Come to me, all of you who are weary and carry heavy burdens, and I will give you rest'" (Matthew 11:28 NLT).

▶ **Abusive Parents**

- **Message received by children**: "Success will be my great escape."

Today, the word *dysfunctional* is used to describe abusive family situations. Dysfunctional families don't foster healthy, nurturing, or warm environments.

- **However**, achievement in areas outside the home becomes a way for children to escape the harsh reality of abuse and neglect within the home.

"My heart took delight in all my labor, and this was the reward for all my toil" (Ecclesiastes 2:10).

▶ Rejecting Parents

- **Message received by children**: "I just have to try harder."

  Children raised by rejecting parents yearn for love, acceptance, and praise. They don't feel loved for who they are and come to believe that performing well will help gain their parents' approval.

- **However**, they personally need to know the unfailing love of God.

  "Though my father and mother forsake me, the Lord will receive me" (Psalm 27:10).

▶ Comparing Parents[14]

- **Message received by children**: "I have to be better than my siblings."

  Each child has individual gifts and abilities. Comparing one child to another is tragic and totally unfair: "Why can't you be more like your sister Susie?" "Why can't you try hard like your brother James?"

- **However**, in this situational setup, bitterness often develops between siblings and resentment builds toward parents.

  "Each one should test their own actions. Then they can take pride in themselves alone, without comparing themselves to someone else" (Galatians 6:4).

▶ Favored Child

- **Message received**: "I have to be responsible and set a good example."

Some parents have excessively high expectations of a certain child whom they view as an extension of themselves. When a parent feels a stronger connection to one child over others for any reason, favoritism can flourish.

- **However**, favoritism, perceived or real, can set up jealousy and competition among siblings and can promote the development of perfectionistic tendencies.

"God does not show favoritism" (Romans 2:11).

▶ Only Child

- **Message received**: "All my family's hopes are wrapped up in me."

Parents of an only child can unknowingly put pressure on their lone successor to be all they hoped to be—and more.

- **However**, with all their "eggs in one basket," they can push and prod their child into perfectionism.

"Fathers, do not exasperate your children; instead, bring them up in the training and instruction of the Lord" (Ephesians 6:4).

▶ Only Male Child

- **Message received**: "The family name is riding on me."

The weight of the family name can feel heavy to a young boy who just wants to enjoy a worry-free childhood. When carrying on the family name obligates a son to be responsible to each member of the ancestral line, many can become perfectionistic.

- **However**, while having a "good name" has much value, living in such a way as to have the favor of the Lord is priceless in value.

"A good name is to be chosen rather than great riches, and favor is better than silver or gold" (Proverbs 22:1 ESV).

▶ **Social Pressure**

- **Message received**: "I need to be at the top!"

Societal pressure to succeed can be unrelenting. Peer pressure to achieve can be overpowering. Such pressure can mold and shape lives for the worse. To rebel against social standards and inner circle norms means certain rejection and instant isolation, motivation enough to develop a tendency toward perfectionism.

- **However**, being pressured to perform will never bring peace to the soul, but humbling the heart before God allows Him to lift us up when the time is right.

"Humble yourselves, therefore, under God's mighty hand, that he may lift you up in due time" (1 Peter 5:6).

"The spur of fame" is what incited the second president of the United States to seek center stage and national acclaim.[15] This John Adams always questioned his reputation and was concerned about his popularity. He was engaged in a relentless pursuit of recognition and distinction, honor and a cherished legacy.

Two images began to emerge on the national scene: the demanding ideals of civic responsibility associated with New England and the comforts that lazily characterized the deep South. Adams made it very clear which direction he was headed at the helm, to occupy the highest office in the land.

The ambitious politician has been aptly described: "He was not one to be seduced by ease."[16] And Adams did his best to make sure his oldest son, John Quincy, also fought against the temptation of folly.

"Folly brings joy to one who has no sense,
but whoever has understanding
keeps a straight course."
(Proverbs 15:21)

The Passion to Push

Those propelled by the passion to achieve, generally experience the push to ...

▶ **Prove** — seeking self-worth

▶ **Produce** — seeking significance

▶ **Perform** — seeking love, admiration, and recognition

▶ **Provide** — seeking to be indispensable

▶ **Protect** — seeking to avoid vulnerability in intimate relationships

▶ **Prosper** — seeking material possessions

▶ **Please** — seeking approval and acceptance

▶ **Perfect** — seeking to be flawless, lacking nothing, needing nothing

Regardless of how impressive a perfectionist's performance or achievement record may be, the Bible presents these sobering words ...

> "What good is it for someone to gain the whole world, yet forfeit their soul?"
> (Mark 8:36)

As John Adams strived to stay in the spotlight of accolades and acclaim, someone he perceived as threatening could steal it and forever cast his legacy into the shadows—namely, *Thomas Jefferson*.[17]

The two historic figures often sparred politically, and the day when Jefferson was to be sworn in as the third president of the United States, Adams made a quick exit from Washington D.C. at four o'clock in the morning. His perfectionistic personality and hunger for achievement, driven in part by his desire to be remembered as the weightier of the two men, even manifested itself on Adams' deathbed with his declaration:

"Jefferson still lives!" But what the 91-year-old second president and statesman didn't know that Independence Day, July 4, 1826, was that his rival, Thomas Jefferson, breathed his last as well. Rather than having his focus on God and heaven, John Adams remained focused on others.

Sadly, it seems he may have been among those who ...

> " ... loved human praise
> more than praise from God."
> (John 12:43)

The Cycle of Perfectionism

Pain
of Past

THE CYCLE OF
PERFECTIONISM

Push to
Perform

Perpetuated
Pain

Promise
of Success

Those bound by the chains of constant achievement generally experience ...

▶ **Pain** from family of origin

- Negative messages
- Performance-based acceptance

▶ **Push** to perform and achieve

- "If I can do enough perfectly, it will ease my pain."
- "If I achieve success, I will feel significant."

▶ **Promise** of success

- "The ultimate achievement is just around the corner."
- "A little more work is all it will take."

▶ **Perpetual** pain

- "I push harder, but I still don't have peace."
- "I feel so guilty—I'm letting people down."

Like the apostle Paul as he reflected on sin, the overachieving perfectionist feels imprisoned by the chains of bondage to a destructive cycle of behavior ...

> "I do not understand what I do.
> For what I want to do I do not do,
> but what I hate I do."
> (Romans 7:15)

WHAT IS the Root Cause of Perfectionism?

The continual finger wagging and focusing on failures induced shame in a young John Quincy Adams and led to a monumental guilt complex.

Every harsh word from his parents, Johnny held as absolute truth. At the age of 10 he wrote, "My thoughts are running after birds' eggs, play and trifles, till I get vexed with myself. Mama has a troublesome task to keep me steady, and I own I am ashamed of myself."[18] The demands of perfectionism did not lead Johnny to rebellion, but resolution—that he could never measure up to their standards.

And even though Johnny became the sixth president of the United States, he never recovered emotionally from the penetrating wounds of perfectionism. He perceived others as viewing him as "a gloomy misanthropist" and "social savage," and in regretful resolution he declared: "I have not the pliability to reform it."[19] In light of these words, it's interesting to read the words of Jesus, *"For the mouth speaks what the heart is full of"* (Matthew 12:34).

The roots of perfectionism can be traced to shame and a sense of insignificance. A traumatic childhood or exposure to overly harsh parenting methods can cause deep feelings of unworthiness or shame. Many cope by trying to hide flaws and striving to be perfect in order to win approval and acceptance.

Some perfectionists even come to take a perverse pride in their pursuit of flawlessness. As a result, they live self-sufficiently and seek to meet their own needs for love, significance, and security.[20] In their own strength they attempt to accomplish what only God can do in them and through them.

However, the Bible says ...

> **"God opposes the proud,
> but gives grace to the humble."**
> **(James 4:6 ESV)**

Three God-Given Inner Needs

In reality, we have all been created with three God-given inner needs: the needs for love, significance, and security.

▶ **Love**—to know that someone is unconditionally committed to our best interest

"My command is this: Love each other as I have loved you" (John 15:12).

▶**Significance**—to know that our lives have meaning and purpose

"I cry out to God Most High, to God who fulfills his purpose for me" (Psalm 57:2 ESV).

▶**Security**—to feel accepted and a sense of belonging

"Whoever fears the LORD has a secure fortress, and for their children it will be a refuge" (Proverbs 14:26).

The Ultimate Need-Meeter

Why did God give us these deep inner needs, knowing that people fail people and self-effort fails us as well?

God gave us these inner needs so that we would come to know Him as our Need-Meeter. Our needs are designed by God to draw us into a deeper dependence on Christ. God did not create any person or position or any amount of power or possessions to meet the deepest needs in our lives. If a person or thing could meet all our needs, we wouldn't need God! The Lord will use circumstances and bring positive people into our lives as an extension of His care and compassion, but ultimately only God can satisfy all the needs of our hearts.

The Bible says ...

"The LORD will guide you always;
he will satisfy your needs in a sun-scorched

**land and will strengthen your frame.
You will be like a well-watered garden,
like a spring whose waters never fail."
(Isaiah 58:11)**

The apostle Paul revealed this truth by first asking, *"What a wretched man I am. Who will rescue me from this body that is subject to death?"* and then by answering his own question in saying it is *"Jesus Christ our Lord!"* (Romans 7:24–25).

All along, the Lord planned to meet our deepest needs for ...

▶ **Love**—*"I [the Lord] have loved you with an everlasting love; I have drawn you with unfailing kindness"* (Jeremiah 31:3).

▶ **Significance**—*"'For I know the plans I have for you,' declares the LORD, 'plans to prosper you and not to harm you, plans to give you hope and a future'"* (Jeremiah 29:11).

▶ **Security**—*"The LORD himself goes before you and will be with you; he will never leave you nor forsake you. Do not be afraid; do not be discouraged"* (Deuteronomy 31:8).

The truth is that our God-given needs for love, significance, and security can be legitimately met in Christ Jesus!

Philippians 4:19 makes it plain ...

"My God will meet all your needs according to the riches of his glory in Christ Jesus."

"I must always appear competent and be able to perform perfectly. Then I can truly accept myself, and others will accept me."

Right Belief of the Recovering Perfectionist

"I can never be perfect or flawless. My competence comes only from the Lord, who empowers me."

"Such confidence we have through Christ before God. Not that we are competent in ourselves to claim anything for ourselves, but our competence comes from God" (2 Corinthians 3:4–5).

WHAT IS God's Perfect Plan for You?

Do you know that the perfect God has a *perfect plan* for your life? Do you *want* God's perfect plan for your life? If so, you need to understand ...

Four Points of God's Plan

#1 God's Purpose for You is *Salvation*.

What was God's motivation in sending Jesus Christ to earth?

To express His love for you by saving you!

The Bible says, *"God so loved the world that he gave his one and only Son, that whoever believes in him shall not perish but have eternal life. For God did not send his Son into the world to condemn the world, but to save the world through him"* (John 3:16–17).

What was Jesus' purpose in coming to earth?

To forgive your sins, to empower you to have victory over sin, and to enable you to live a fulfilled life!

Jesus said, *"I have come that they may have life, and that they may have it more abundantly"* (John 10:10 NKJV).

#2 Your Problem is *Sin*.

What exactly is sin?

Sin is living independently of God's standard— knowing what is right, but choosing what is wrong.

The Bible says, *"If anyone, then, knows the good they ought to do and doesn't do it, it is sin for them"* (James 4:17).

What is the major consequence of sin?

Spiritual death, eternal separation from God.

Scripture states, *"Your iniquities* [sins] *have separated you from your God" (*Isaiah 59:2).

"The wages of sin is death, but the gift of God is eternal life in Christ Jesus our Lord" (Romans 6:23).

#3 God's Provision for You is the *Savior*.

Can anything remove the penalty for sin?

Yes! Jesus died on the cross to personally pay the penalty for your sins.

The Bible says, *"God demonstrates his own love for us in this: While we were still sinners, Christ died for us"* (Romans 5:8).

What is the solution to being separated from God?

Belief in (entrusting your life to) Jesus Christ as the only way to God the Father.

Jesus says, *"I am the way and the truth and the life. No one comes to the Father except through me"* (John 14:60).

"Believe in the Lord Jesus, and you will be saved" (Acts 16:31).

#4 Your Part is *Surrender.*

Give Christ control of your life, entrusting yourself to Him.

"Jesus said to his disciples, 'Whoever wants to be my disciple must deny themselves and take up their cross [die to your own self-rule] *and follow me. For whoever wants to save their life will lose it, but whoever loses their life for me will find it. What good will it be for someone to gain the whole world, yet forfeit their soul?'"* (Matthew 16:24–26).

Place your faith in (rely on) Jesus Christ as your personal Lord and Savior and reject your "good works" as a means of earning God's approval.

"It is by grace you have been saved, through faith— and this is not from yourselves, it is the gift of God—not by works, so that no one can boast" (Ephesians 2:8–9).

The moment you choose to receive Jesus as your Lord and Savior—entrusting your life to Him—His Spirit lives inside you. Then you receive power to live the fulfilled life God has planned for you. If you want to be fully forgiven by God and become the person God created you to be, you can tell Him in a simple, heartfelt prayer like this:

PRAYER OF SALVATION

*"God, I want a real relationship with You.
I admit that many times I've chosen to go
my own way instead of Your way.
Please forgive me for my sins.
Jesus, thank You for dying on the cross to
pay the penalty for my sins.
Come into my life to be my Lord
and my Savior.
Change me from the inside out and make
me the person You created me to be.
In Your holy name I pray. Amen."*

WHAT CAN YOU NOW EXPECT?

If you sincerely prayed this prayer, know that you don't have to be perfect or achieve success in the world's eyes because the Bible says, *"For by one sacrifice he has made perfect forever those who are being made holy"* (Hebrews 10:14).

STEPS TO SOLUTION

Many people today live in a society that values exceptional efforts and extraordinary accomplishments where people push themselves unreasonably hard to achieve the admiration of others.

How far away the priorities of many have moved from the priorities of God! True success—and lasting peace of mind—come from aligning your values and your expectations with God's, which are found in His Word. Rather than seeking the approval of other people, seek the grace of God. Rather than seeking outward beauty, seek inner beauty. Focus on changing your character rather than altering your appearance.

Remember Jesus' words ...

"But let your adorning be the hidden person of the heart with the imperishable beauty of a gentle and quiet spirit, which in God's sight is very precious."
(1 Peter 3:4 ESV)

Only in God will you find unconditional love, true significance, and eternal security—the longings of perfectionists. And it is only by His grace that you can receive them through faith in Him, as the apostle Paul reminds us ...

KEY VERSE TO MEMORIZE

"For it is by grace you have been saved, through faith—and this is not from yourselves, it is the gift of God—not by works, so that no one can boast."
(Ephesians 2:8–9)

Key Passage to Read

PHILIPPIANS 3:1–14

In Philippians 3 Paul explains how he spent his life striving for religious perfection. He confesses he was a *"Hebrew of Hebrews,"* was focusing on *"righteousness based on the law,"* and was driven to be *"faultless"* (verses 5 and 6). Yet in coming to know the Son of God, Paul had a change of mind and a change of heart.

Now he dismisses his previous achievements as *"garbage"* (verse 8) because he has come to know the *truly perfect* man: Jesus Christ. Paul concludes that he humbly strives to experience his worth through Christ, *"not that I have already obtained all this"* (verse 12), yet he presses on, completely convinced he is now walking the right path.

Paul the Perfectionist

Before accepting Christ and while living in his own strength, Paul ...

▶ **Placed** confidence in his own abilities (v. 4)

▶ **Prided** himself in his elite status and heritage (v. 5)

▶ **Practiced** legalism (v. 5)

▶ **Pushed** toward his goals with zeal (v. 6)

▶ **Persecuted** Jews he considered enemies of Judaism (v. 6)

▶ **Presumed** himself righteous through personal achievement (v. 6)

Paul the Pursuer of Excellence

After dying to self and while living in Christ's strength, Paul ...

▶ **Put** no confidence in himself, but gloried in Christ Jesus (v. 3)

▶ **Perceived** personal gain to be loss (v. 7)

▶ **Pronounced** all things to be garbage compared to knowing Christ (v. 8)

▶ **Pursued** knowing Christ as his highest goal (v. 8)

▶ **Professed** no personal righteousness from performance (v. 9)

▶ **Prescribed** righteousness from God through faith in Christ (v. 9)

- ▶ **Purposed** to experience Christ, His resurrection power, His sufferings, and His death (vv. 10–11)

- ▶ **Proclaimed** no perfection in himself (v. 12)

- ▶ **Pressed** on to maturity in Christ (vv. 13–14)

HOW TO Have a Transformed Life

REACHING THE TARGET: TRANSFORMATION!

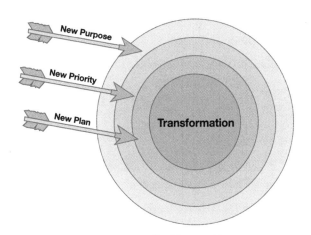

THE FREEDOM FORMULA

	A New Purpose
+	A New Priority
+	A New Plan
	A Transformed Life

Target #1—A New Purpose: God's purpose for me is to be conformed to the character of Christ.

> *"Those God foreknew he also predestined to be conformed to the image of his Son ... "* (Romans 8:29).

- "I'll do whatever it takes to be conformed to the character of Christ."

Target #2—A New Priority: God's priority for me is to change my thinking.

> *"Do not conform to the pattern of this world, but be transformed by the renewing of your mind"* (Romans 12:2).

- "I'll do whatever it takes to line up my thinking with God's thinking.

Target #3—A New Plan: God's plan for me is to rely on Christ's strength, not my strength, to be all He created me to be.

> *"I can do all things through him who strengthens me"* (Philippians 4:13 ESV).

- "I'll do whatever it takes to fulfill His plan in His strength."

My Personalized Plan

My quest is to seek the approval of God rather than people, to view my mistakes as grace-filled opportunities for growth and maturity, and to live out the truth that God accepts and approves of me as I am today and as I will be every day hereafter.

In this quest, I will ...

▶ **Target My Tendencies**

I entreat you, Heavenly Father, *"Search me, God, and know my heart; test me and know my anxious thoughts. See if there is any offensive way in me, and lead me in the way everlasting"* (Psalm 139:23–24).

"Lord, reveal any demanding ideals, any **possible pockets of perfectionism** that have become a blind spot of unrealistic expectations to me as I answer the following questions."[21]

	Yes	No
Is **orderliness** necessary for me to relax?	❑	❑
Has **cleanliness** become an obsession?	❑	❑
Do **family members** have to be exemplary?	❑	❑
Is **punctuality** a must?	❑	❑
Does my **work** always have to be praiseworthy?	❑	❑

	Yes	No
Must my **appearance** always be immaculate?	☐	☐
Does my specific **skill** have to be exceptional?	☐	☐
Do I expect other people to meet my **personal high standards**?	☐	☐

If I respond with yes to some of these questions, then I will follow this instruction ...

> "Cast all your anxiety on him
> because he cares for you."
> (1 Peter 5:7)

▶ **Face My Feelings**[22]

In my quest for freedom, I will pour out my heart to God:

"Relieve the troubles of my heart and free me from my anguish" (Psalm 25:17).

I will ...

- **Recognize** my longing for acceptance.

    Read the Psalms to find passages describing my deepest feelings, and then express them to God.

- **Allow** myself to feel the pain of my past.

    Find someone with whom I can pray and share my hurt feelings from childhood—feelings that continue to impact me today.

- **Extend** compassion to those in my life who have given me only conditional love.

  Realize that they have probably treated me the same way they were treated.

- **Let go** of my resentment toward those who have hurt me.

  Give these feelings to the Lord and experience His peace and healing in my life.

- **Release** my anger and pain to God and make a conscious choice to forgive.

  Pray, thanking the Lord for removing this heavy burden from me.

The Bible assures me ...

"The Lord is close to the brokenhearted and saves those who are crushed in spirit." (Psalm 34:18)

▶ **Commit to Change**

On my path to freedom, I will remember that I am not alone.

"Since we are surrounded by such a great cloud of witnesses, let us throw off everything that hinders and the sin that so easily entangles. And let us run with perseverance the race marked out for us" (Hebrews 12:1).

I will ...

- **Know** that change is difficult, but well worth the effort.

Choose to be satisfied with less than perfection, focusing on the peace I will gain.

- **Cease** all comparisons between myself and others.

  Replace my extreme standards for more realistic, reasonable expectations of myself and others.

- **Take** responsibility for making the decision to do what is right for me even in the face of opposition.

  Set beneficial personal goals based on healthy, legitimate needs.

- **Cultivate** the ability to say "no" at times to people and to projects.

  Confront my fears, asking myself, "If I am less than perfect, what is the worst that can happen and what good can come from it?"

- **Appreciate** the lessons my mistakes can teach me and find humor in my human errors.

  Lighten up and realize that I can learn more from my mistakes than my successes.

In committing to change, it is essential that I have the right goal.

**"We make it our goal to please him [God] ... For we must all appear before the judgment seat of Christ, so that each of us may receive what is due us for the things done while in the body, whether good or bad."
(2 Corinthians 5:9–10)**

▶ Master My Mind

While pursuing priceless freedom, I will heed the words of the apostle Paul ...

"Do not conform to the pattern of this world, but be transformed by the renewing of your mind Then you will be able to test and approve what God's will is—his good, pleasing and perfect will" (Romans 12:2).

I will ...

- **Eliminate** my "all-or-nothing" thinking and be flexible.

- **Keep** a daily journal of negative thoughts about myself and replace them with positive statements based on biblical truth. "Thank You, God, for Your unconditional love for me."

- **Tell** myself the truth by memorizing and appropriating God's "messages of grace."

   "I commit you to God and to the word of his grace, which can build you up and give you an inheritance among all those who are sanctified" (Acts 20:32).

- **Pray** daily for God's intervention to help me take charge of my thoughts.

I will remember that I am in a battle for my mind and must use the weapons designed by God.

**"The weapons we fight with
are not the weapons of the world.
On the contrary, they have divine power**

to demolish strongholds.
We demolish arguments
and every pretension that sets itself up
against the knowledge of God,
and we take captive every thought
to make it obedient to Christ."
(2 Corinthians 10:4–5)

▶ Lose My Life

In following after my God-given freedom, I will fulfill its costly formula ...

" ... *whoever loses their life for me and for the gospel will save it*" (Mark 8:35).

I will ...

- **Surrender** my demand to have my own way.

- **Let go** of my right to live life out of my own resources.

- **Trust** God to meet all of my needs.

- **Submit** myself to the prompting of the Holy Spirit.

- **Choose** to live every moment of every day in dependence on Christ.

I will remember to rest in the assurance that ...

"His divine power has given us everything
we need for a godly life through our
knowledge of him who called us by his own
glory and goodness. Through these he
has given us his very great and precious
promises, so that through them

you may participate in the divine nature,
having escaped the corruption
in the world caused by evil desires."
(2 Peter 1:3–4)

▶ Grow in Grace

In my resolve to attain my freedom, I will remember that my God, the God of all grace, wants to give me a heart full of grace—grace toward myself and others. Grace involves unmerited favor, undeserved care, unearned love. I will allow the Spirit of Christ within me to produce the fruit of His Spirit through me.

"The fruit of the Spirit is love, joy, peace, patience, kindness, goodness, faithfulness, gentleness, self-control; against such things there is no law" (Galatians 5:22–23 ESV).

- **Love**—"Lord, I will look at others through Your eyes of love and learn to love unconditionally."

- **Joy**—"Lord, I will find joy in the little things and learn to laugh at my own mistakes."

- **Peace**—"Lord, I will have peace in the midst of my storms, knowing the Prince of Peace lives within me."

- **Patience**—"Lord, I will be patient with others because You are patient with me."

- **Kindness**—"Lord, I will be kind with my words and refrain from criticizing others."

- **Goodness**—"Lord, I will look at the good in others and refuse to focus on the flaws."

- **Faithfulness**—"Lord, thank You for being faithful to me even when I am unfaithful to You, to others, and to myself."

- **Gentleness**—"Lord, I will be gentle with the hearts of others just as You are gentle with me."

- **Self-control**—"Lord, I will give up trying to be perfect and will give You control of my life."

As I grow in God's grace, I will be assured ...

"God is able to bless you abundantly,
so that in all things at all times,
having all that you need,
you will abound in every good work."
(2 Corinthians 9:8)

One way to help perfectionists manage time is to encourage them to think of themselves as a bank account. If they keep making time withdrawals without making time deposits, they're headed for bankruptcy—*physically*, *spiritually*, and *emotionally*.

Maintaining a healthy, balanced "time account" means making deposits of time into their personal lives, starting with setting aside 15 minutes to an hour each day for themselves. The time can be spent any way they choose, but it has to be restful and unrelated to work.

Feelings of restlessness, boredom, or even depression can accompany initial attempts to deprogram from work, but the end result actually will be improved job performance, strengthened relationships, and renewed self-respect.

God's Word addresses the proper use of time ...

" ... the wise heart will know
the proper time and procedure.
For there is a proper time and procedure
for every matter, though a person may be
weighed down by misery."
(Ecclesiastes 8:5–6)

As you try to wisely handle time, eliminate the thought that working day and night is sacrificial and that doing the job "perfectly" is spiritual.

Take to heart King Solomon's words ...

> "In vain you rise early and stay up late,
> toiling for food to eat—
> for he grants sleep to those he loves."
> (Psalm 127:2)

▶ **Spend time with God** in His Word and in prayer.

"I delight in your decrees; I will not neglect your word" (Psalm 119:16).

▶ **Write a "To Do" list** daily—preferably the evening before. Make it realistic and reflective of your priorities.

"To humans belong the plans of the heart, but from the LORD comes the proper answer of the tongue. Commit to the LORD whatever you do, and he will establish your plans" (Proverbs 16:1, 3).

▶ **List your detailed plans** in order of importance. Remember the benefit of doing them with diligence.

"The plans of the diligent lead to profit as surely as haste leads to poverty" (Proverbs 21:5).

▶ **Establish a starting and finishing time** for each task. Stick to your time schedule so one activity does not take time allotted to another.

"There is a time for everything, and a season for every activity under the heavens" (Ecclesiastes 3:1).

▶ **Set parameters** on having an open-door policy to ensure "alone time." Guard your time with God just as Jesus protected His time with the Father.

"After he had dismissed them, he went up on a mountainside by himself to pray. Later that night, he was there alone" (Matthew 14:23).

▶ **Set aside specific time** for family, for friends, and for yourself. There is great reward in planning activities with loved ones.

"Those who plan what is good find love and faithfulness" (Proverbs 14:22).

HOW TO Find Freedom from Perfectionism

God has called you to an honest day's work, but not to achievement addiction.

Consider Jesus' example: He fed the hungry, calmed the storm, healed the sick, raised the dead. But still He *"withdrew to lonely places and prayed"* (Luke 5:16), in spite of the throngs still seeking Him out—still wanting His touch. He knew His need for time with His Father, to be at one with the Father, to be in the will of the Father and for the glory of the Father—not His own glory.

And it's the same for you. God is calling you to slow down, to spend time with Him, to draw on His strength and to work neither for recognition nor for glory, but to work for *His glory*.

By following Jesus' example, you will ...

> **"Do nothing out of selfish ambition
> or vain conceit." (Philippians 2:3)**

In your quest for **FREEDOM** ...

FULFILL your God-given call to live under grace, not under law.

▶ Realize God's favor is freely given and cannot be earned through achievement.

▶ Operate under God's principle of grace and gratitude, not fear and compulsion.

▶ Remember to pursue freedom, not enslavement.

"Formerly, when you did not know God, you were slaves to those who by nature are not gods. But now that you know God—or rather are known by God—how is it that you are turning back to those weak and miserable forces? Do you wish to be enslaved by them all over again?" (Galatians 4:8–9).

RELEASE your burden of guilt to God.

▶ Forgive yourself for not being perfect.

▶ Learn the difference between true guilt, based on harboring unconfessed sin, and false guilt, based on feeling condemned for forgiven sins or for false accusations.

▶ Remember, Jesus died to give you a clear conscience so that you might not be hindered in drawing near to God.

"Let us draw near to God with a sincere heart and with the full assurance that faith brings, having our hearts sprinkled to cleanse us from a guilty conscience and having our bodies washed with pure water" (Hebrews 10:22).

ELIMINATE your need to please others, and focus on pleasing God.

▶ Make it your ambition to stop pursuing self-promoting achievement and start pursuing that which pleases God.

▶ Study God's Word to learn what God values and what attitudes and actions are pleasing to Him.

▶ Remember, the Lord's desires for your life can be summed up in three requirements:

"And what does the LORD require of you? To act justly and to love mercy and to walk humbly with your God" (Micah 6:8).

ENLARGE your time for rest, recreation, and communion with the Lord.

▶ Learn to pause, worship, and reflect on God during the day.

▶ Slow down, rest, and appreciate the small things in life, the things too priceless for money to buy, but regularly taken for granted.

▶ Remember, there is but one place of true rest.

"My soul waits in silence for God only; from Him is my salvation" (Psalm 62:1 NASB).

DECIDE to acknowledge your personal feelings honestly and release all resentment.

▶ Acknowledge resentment; face and release any feelings of hurt toward your parents or others for not helping meet your needs for love, significance, and security.

▶ Become more compassionate toward others with similar struggles.

▶ Remember, God places a high value on honesty and forgiveness.

"The godless in heart harbor resentment; even when he fetters them, they do not cry for help" (Job 36:13).

OBEY your Savior's mandate to live by the law of love rather than by the law of fear.

▶ Let love become the motive behind all of your actions.

▶ Let love free you to become involved in the lives of others.

▶ Remember, the remedy for fear is love.

"There is no fear in love. But perfect love drives out fear, because fear has to do with punishment. The one who fears is not made perfect in love" (1 John 4:18).

MAINTAIN your sense of significance and satisfy your need for security by finding your identity in Christ.

▶ Realize, it is the Lord who establishes your worthiness and gives your life significance and security.

▶ Understand, you must die to self before Christ can live His life through you.

▶ Remember, you have a new life in Christ, and you now belong to Him.

"I have been crucified with Christ and I no longer live, but Christ lives in me. The life I now live in the body, I live by faith in the Son of God, who loved me and gave himself for me" (Galatians 2:20).

HOW TO Overcome Obsessive Thoughts and Compulsive Actions

In most cases, the goal of treatment for Obsessive Compulsive Disorder (OCD) is not to totally eliminate symptoms but to reduce them to the point they no longer disrupt a person's ability to function in everyday life.

Most of those treated for OCD by specially trained professionals improve after receiving cognitive behavioral therapy over a period of roughly 10 weeks. This therapy has the potential of literally "retraining the brain" through practicing repetitive behavior over an extended period of time.

The need for "retraining" is experienced by everyone according to the words of the apostle Paul ...

> " ... be made new in the attitude of your minds ... " (Ephesians 4:23)

Three-Pronged Treatment for OCD[23]

▶ **Behavioral Therapy**

- Introduce exposure on a gradual basis to obsessions or fear-producing objects. This process is called "desensitization."

- Increase exposure over a period of time to objects normally avoided.

- Inhibit behaviors aimed at reducing anxiety when exposed to objects that are being avoided.

- Include in treatment those family members whose lives are being disrupted by the person's OCD behavior or those enabling the behavior.

▶ **Cognitive Therapy**

- Realize that unintentional, intrusive, persistent thoughts and urges are the result of OCD, and their impact can be controlled and regulated.

- Recognize that OCD and its resulting thoughts and urges are likely related to a chemical imbalance in the brain over which the individual has no direct control.

(The neurotransmitter serotonin appears to play a significant role in OCD.)

- Redirect thoughts and actions away from obsessive and compulsive thoughts and urges by intentionally setting the mind on something else and engaging in a different related behavior.

- Reaffirm the truth that obsessive/compulsive thoughts and urges have no basis in reality, and do not need to be entertained.

▶ **Medication**

- Selective serotonin reuptake inhibitors (SSRIs) dramatically impact the symptoms of OCD, have fewer side effects than previously used antidepressants, and are used by practicing family physicians.

- Side effects sometimes experienced by users of SSRIs include insomnia, akathisia (motor restlessness), nausea, and diarrhea.

Cognitive behavioral therapy plus SSRIs is the current preferred treatment for people with severe OCD, while cognitive behavioral therapy alone can be effective for individuals with milder cases of OCD. Group therapy can also be helpful in providing support, encouragement, and can help in decreasing feelings of isolation.

"Plans are established by
seeking advice ... obtain guidance."
(Proverbs 20:18)

For perfectionists, it can be considered a paradox. The imperfect strive for perfectionism in themselves and in others. When impossible standards aren't met it leads to self-dissatisfaction and disapproval of others. But the Lord, on the other hand, who is flawless and never, ever fails, totally accepts those who belong to Him despite their repeated imperfections.

Perfectionists should embrace the comforting assurances of acceptance in Scripture and extend to others the same acceptance they receive in Christ.

> **"May the God who gives endurance and encouragement give you the same attitude of mind toward each other that Christ Jesus had."**
> **(Romans 15:5)**

The Bible is filled with true stories about people who are far from perfect. Even God's greatest servants had flaws, experienced failure, and at times collapsed in what they deemed to be final defeat. But God's unmatchable grace, picked them back up time and time again, and empowered them to soar to even greater heights of service.

The challenging question is: How do you free yourself from the chains of perfectionism? According to God's Word, you gain freedom by claiming your new identity in Christ. God sent his Son, Jesus, to die for you so that your sins *and imperfections* would forever be forgiven. Jesus met the standard for perfection—and when you trust in Him by turning your life over to Him, you receive His righteousness—and you are fully accepted.

" ... He chose us in Him [Christ] before the foundation of the world ... as sons by Jesus Christ to Himself, according to the good pleasure of His will ... by which He made us accepted in the Beloved."
(Ephesians 1:3–6 NKJV)

As you grow in maturity, you are set free from the shackles of perfectionism—free to grow in truly amazing grace. Embracing grace enables you to accept God's undeserved, unmerited, unearned favor despite your imperfections.

Each of the following points will help you line up with the Lord's thinking. Accept His acceptance as you ...

▶ **Evaluate** your extremes.

Usually a perfectionist is rigid, harsh, and hard on others.

But the Bible says you are to, *"Let your gentleness be evident to all"* (Philippians 4:5).

▶ **Expect** discomfort.

Change is always uncomfortable. Changing certain thought patterns and the way you've acted over a period of years can be unsettling.

But the Bible says you are to, *"put off your old self, which is being corrupted by its deceitful desires; to be made new in the attitude of your minds; and to put on the new self, created to be like God in true righteousness and holiness"* (Ephesians 4:22–24).

▶ **Stop** comparing.

Comparison leads to either feelings of inferiority or feelings of superiority.

But the Bible says we are to, *"not dare to classify or compare ourselves with some who commend themselves. When they measure themselves by themselves and compare themselves with themselves, they are not wise"* (2 Corinthians 10:12).

▶ **Abolish** expectations!

Identify unrealistic expectations of yourself and of others and remove them.

The Bible says we are to, *"Be devoted to one another in love. Honor one another above yourselves"* (Romans 12:10).

▶ **Laugh** at your mistakes.

How? Learn to find humorous aspects of failure. After all, everyone experiences it and rarely is it ever fatal. Satan would use your mistakes to crush your spirit.

But the Bible says we are to remember, *"All the days of the oppressed are wretched, but the cheerful heart has a continual feast"* (Proverbs 15:15), and *"A cheerful heart is good medicine, but a crushed spirit dries up the bones"* (Proverbs 17:22).

▶ **Practice** patience—it's a virtue!

Listen to your language—does it compliment or criticize others? And is your tone accepting or condemning? Impatience leads to unwholesome speech.

But the Bible says you are to, *"not let any unwholesome talk come out of your mouths, but only what is helpful for building others up according to their needs, that it may benefit those who listen"* (Ephesians 4:29).

▶ **Just** say *no*!

On occasion, Christ said no to others. If you are going to be Christlike, you need to know when to say no to others in order to say yes to God. People pleasers do not know they have the right to say *no*.

But they can learn from Jesus' example: *"Jesus' brothers said to him, 'Leave Galilee and go to Judea, so that your disciples there may see the works you do.' ... 'You go to the festival. I am not going up to this festival, because my time has not yet fully come'"* (John 7:3, 8).

▶ **Get** a grip on grace!

Pray that you will continue to grow in grace, giving by manifesting unmerited, undeserved, unearned favor to those who don't meet your expectations. Extending godly, unconditional grace is not natural in the flesh and contradicts human nature; therefore, we are dependent on the Lord.

But the Bible says you are to, *"Grow in the grace and knowledge of our Lord and Savior Jesus Christ. To him be glory both now and forever!"* (2 Peter 3:18).

▶ **Don't** be so demanding!

Ditch your demands: *I should have, I ought to,* and *I have to.* When you grow up under a list of harsh rules, it is difficult to live under a different standard.

But the Bible says you are to remember, *"You who are trying to be justified by the law have been alienated from Christ; you have fallen away from grace"* (Galatians 5:4).

▶ **Be** accepting.

Because God accepted you when you didn't deserve it, you can accept others when they don't deserve it. The world will tell you to reject those who reject you.

But the Bible says you are to, *"Accept one another, then, just as Christ accepted you, in order to bring praise to God"* (Romans 15:7).

▶ **Condemn** no more!

God doesn't focus on your flaws. Why should you? Don't set yourself up as a higher judge than God! Satan will try to keep your flaws in your face.

But the Bible says you are to remember, *"There is now no condemnation for those who are in Christ Jesus"* (Romans 8:1).

▶ **Cancel** your performance!

Exchange your push to perform for Christ's performing His perfect work through you, because in your own strength you are sure to fail.

But the Bible says you can be fully assured, *"I can do all things through him who strengthens me"* (Philippians 4:13 ESV).

> *God gives you significance just by*
> *making you His child,*
> *not by asking you to be perfect.*
> *Instead of focusing on your flaws,*
> *God focuses on your future,*
> *your identity is in Him.*
>
> —June Hunt

SCRIPTURES TO MEMORIZE

While the **Spirit** of God convicts us of sin and our need for salvation, does trying to accomplish His will through the **flesh** earn favor with God?

*"Are you so foolish? After beginning by means of the **Spirit**, are you now trying to finish by means of the **flesh**?"* (Galatians 3:3)

Although **Christ has set us free** from the penalty of sin, don't we still need to try to keep the dos and don'ts of the law perfectly?

*"It is for freedom that **Christ has set us free**. Stand firm, then, and do not let yourselves be burdened again by a yoke of slavery."* (Galatians 5:1)

Is it **wise** to **compare ourselves** with others?

*"We do not dare to classify or **compare ourselves** with some who commend themselves. When they measure themselves by themselves and compare themselves with themselves, they are not **wise**."* (2 Corinthians 10:12)

How can I not **look at** the imperfections of others? They draw my **attention**.

*"Why do you **look at** the speck of sawdust in your brother's eye and pay no **attention** to the plank in your own eye?"* (Matthew 7:3)

How can the **grace** of Jesus be **sufficient** when, in truth, I am weak?

*"My **grace** is **sufficient** for you, for my power is made perfect in weakness."* (2 Corinthians 12:9)

Won't many moral people be **saved** based on having done so many good **works**?

*"It is by grace you have been **saved**, through faith —and this is not from yourselves, it is the gift of God —not by **works**, so that no one can boast."* (Ephesians 2:8–9)

If someone is **righteous** in the eyes of God, do they always do **what is right**?

*"There is no one on earth who is **righteous**, no one who does **what is right** and never sins."* (Ecclesiastes 7:20)

At times my perfectionism leads to pridefulness. How can I be **humble** instead of **proud**?

*"All of you, clothe yourselves with humility toward one another, because, 'God opposes the **proud** but shows favor to the **humble**.' Humble yourselves, therefore, under God's mighty hand, that he may lift you up in due time."* (1 Peter 5:5–6)

Does serving Christ include **trying to win the approval of people**?

*"Am I now **trying to win the approval of** human beings, or of God? Or am I trying to please **people**? If I were still trying to please people, I would not be a servant of Christ." (Galatians 1:10)*

How can I fight being a perfectionist when I know I'm **competent** in many areas?

*"Not that we are **competent** in ourselves to claim anything for ourselves, but our competence comes from God."* (2 Corinthians 3:5)

NOTES

1. Merriam-Webster, *Merriam-Webster Online Dictionary* (Springfield, MA: Merriam-Webster, 2005), Merriam-webster.com, s.v. "Perfection."

2. W. E. Vine, Merrill F. Unger, and William White, Jr., *Vine's Expository Dictionary of Biblical Words* (Nashville: Thomas Nelson, 1985), s.v. "Perfect."

3. Vine, Unger, and White, Jr., *Vine's Expository Dictionary of Biblical Words*, s.v. "Perfect."

4. Vine, Unger, and White, Jr., *Vine's Expository Dictionary of Biblical Words*, s.v. "Perfect."

5. American Psychiatric Association, *Diagnostic and Statistical Manual of Mental Disorders,* 4th ed., text revision (Washington, D.C.: American Psychiatric Association, 2000), 725.

6. Greg Moran, "A Champion Comes Back" *Tennis Server,* http://www.tennisserver.com/mortal/mortal_06_11.html.

7. Moran, "A Champion Comes Back."

8. David A. Stoop, *Living with a Perfectionist* (Nashville: Thomas Nelson, 1987), 44–45.

9. Scott J. Behson, "Work-Family Comes to the World of Sports" *The Industrial/Organizational Psychologist,* April, 1999, 51–56.

10. Miriam Adderholdt and Jan Goldberg, *Perfectionism: What's Bad About Being Too Good?* rev. and updated ed. (Minneapolis, MN: Free Spirit, 1999), 4–5; Stoop, *Living with a Perfectionist,* 30.

11. Robert V. Remini, *John Quincy Adams* (New York: Times Books, 2002), 2–3.

12. Remini, *John Quincy Adams,* 3.

13. Stoop, *Living with a Perfectionist,* 72–76.

14. Stoop, *Living with a Perfectionist,* 54.

15. John P. Diggins, *John Adams* (New York: Times Books, 2003), 1.

16. Diggins, *John Adams*, 10.

17. Diggins, *John Adams*, 2, 5.

18. Remini, *John Quincy Adams*, 5.

19. Diggins, *John Adams*, 3.

20. Lawrence J. Crabb, Jr., *Understanding People: Deep Longings for Relationship*, Ministry Resources Library (Grand Rapids: Zondervan, 1987), 15–16; Robert S. McGee, *The Search for Significance*, 2nd ed. (Houston, TX: Rapha, 1990), 27–30.

21. Stoop, *Living with a Perfectionist*, 26–28.

22. Stoop, *Living with a Perfectionist*, 112–121.

23. Healthwise, "Obsesive-Compulsive Disorder (OCD)-Topic Overview" (n.p.: WebMD, June 21, 2010), http://www.webmd.com/anxiety-panic/tc/obsessive-compulsive-disorder-ocd-topic-overview?page=2.

June Hunt's HOPE FOR THE HEART minibooks are biblically-based, and full of practical advice that is relevant, spiritually-fulfilling and wholesome.

HOPE FOR THE HEART TITLES

www.aspirepress.com